OLD GIT Wit

QUIPS AND QUOTES FOR THE YOUNG AT HEART

RICHARD BENSON

summersdale

OLD GIT WIT

First published in 2006
Reprinted in 2007, 2008, 2009, 2010, 2014
This edition copyright © Summersdale Publishers Ltd, 2013

Illustrations © Roger Roberts and © Shutterstock

Summersdale Publishers Ltd
46 West Street
Chichester
West Sussex
PO19 1RP
UK

www.summersdale.com

Printed and bound by CPI Group (UK) Ltd, Croydon, CR0 4YY

ISBN: 978-1-84953-461-1

Substantial discounts on bulk quantities of Summersdale books are available to corporations, professional associations and other organisations. For details contact Nicky Douglas by telephone: +44 (0) 1243 756902, fax: +44 (0) 1243 786300 or email: nicky@summersdale.com.

CONTENTS

EDITOR'S NOTE

Life expectancy has soared in recent years, with experts telling us that centenarians will soon be as commonplace as two-car households. Old age is here to stay – so put on your specs and pay attention!

However many golden years you've clocked up, or even if you've got it all to look forward to, popular personalities from literature, screen, politics and more share their witty observations on seniority. Typically cynical old grumps including Winston Churchill and Bob Hope moan as only seasoned veterans of life can, while Shakespeare laments an age when one becomes 'blasted with antiquity'. Yet it is good to know that 'Grey Power' is hanging in there to celebrate all that makes elderliness exceptional. Philosopher Bertrand Russell ponders the advantages of white hair while both Picasso and Brigitte Bardot talk of old age as a 'ripening'.

From advice on side-stepping the age question in the Birthdays section to priceless tips in Secrets of Longevity, there are hilarious remarks to sweeten the pill of every aspect of old age. And with contributors ranging from young'uns like Drew Barrymore and Harry Hill to the longest-living human being officially recorded, Jeanne Calment (122 at the time of her death), it's worth taking the time to laugh at the wrinkles and forgetfulness.

As Maurice Chevalier so aptly put it, old age is not so bad when you consider the alternative.

ACCEPTING OLD AGE

Old age is not so bad
when you consider
the alternative.

MAURICE CHEVALIER, FRENCH MUSICAL-COMEDY STAR

When it comes to old age we're all in the same boat, only some of us have been aboard a little longer.

LEO PROBST

What's a man's age? He must
hurry more, that's all;
Cram in a day what his
youth took a year to hold.

ROBERT BROWNING, BRITISH POET

●●●

Old age is like a plane
flying through a storm.
Once you're aboard, there's
nothing you can do.

GOLDA MEIR, ONE OF THE FOUNDERS OF
ISRAEL AND PRIME MINISTER

Eventually you will reach a point
when you stop lying about your
age and start bragging about it.

WILL ROGERS, AMERICAN COMEDIAN AND ACTOR

———•••———

Getting old is a fascinating
thing. The older you get, the
older you want to get.

KEITH RICHARDS, BRITISH ROCK MUSICIAN

———•••———

At middle age the soul should
be opening up like a rose, not
closing up like a cabbage.

JOHN ANDREW HOLMES, AMERICAN PHYSICIAN AND WRITER

I always add a year to myself,
so I'm prepared for my next
birthday. So when I was
39, I was already 40.

NICOLAS CAGE, AMERICAN ACTOR

———— •••• ————

Don't let ageing get you down.
It's too hard to get back up.

JOHN WAGNER, AMERICAN-BORN BRITISH COMIC WRITER

BENEFITS OF OLD AGE

Old age takes away
what we've inherited
and gives us what
we've earned.

GERALD BRENAN, BRITISH WRITER

We don't grow older,
we grow riper.

PABLO PICASSO, SPANISH PAINTER AND SCULPTOR

I have enjoyed greatly the second blooming that comes when you finish the life of the emotions and of personal relations; and suddenly find – at the age of 50, say – that a whole new life has opened before you, filled with things you can think about, study, or read about... It is as if a fresh sap of ideas and thoughts was rising in you.

AGATHA CHRISTIE, BRITISH NOVELIST AND PLAYWRIGHT

———— •◦• ————

One good thing about getting older is that if you're getting married, the phrase 'till death do us part' doesn't sound so horrible. It only means about 10 or 15 years and not the eternity it used to mean.

JOY BEHAR, AMERICAN COMEDIAN AND TALK SHOW HOST

One of the best parts of growing older? You can flirt all you like since you've become harmless.

LIZ SMITH, BRITISH ACTRESS

●●●

The age of a woman doesn't mean a thing. The best tunes are played on the oldest fiddles.

RALPH WALDO EMERSON, AMERICAN WRITER

●●●

Autumn is really the best of the seasons; and I'm not sure that old age isn't the best part of life.

C. S. LEWIS, IRISH SCHOLAR AND NOVELIST

As you grow old, you lose interest in sex, your friends drift away, and your children often ignore you. There are other advantages, of course, but these are the outstanding ones.

RICHARD NEEDHAM, EARL OF KILMOREY, BRITISH POLITICIAN

—•●•—

The more sand has escaped from the hourglass of our life, the clearer we should see through it.

NICCOLO MACHIAVELLI, FLORENTINE PATRIOT AND WRITER

The great thing about getting older is that you don't lose all the other ages you've been.

MADELEINE L'ENGLE, AMERICAN WRITER

Old age, believe me, is a good and pleasant thing. It is true you are gently shouldered off the stage, but then you are given such a comfortable front stall as spectator.

JANE HARRISON, BRITISH CLASSICAL SCHOLAR AND WRITER

I've got cheekier with
age. You can get away
with murder when
you're 71 years old.
People just think
I'm a silly old fool.

BERNARD MANNING, BRITISH COMEDIAN

The great comfort of turning
49 is the realisation that you
are now too old to die young.

PAUL DICKSON, AMERICAN WRITER

One of the good things about
getting older is you find you're
more interesting than most
of the people you meet.

LEE MARVIN, AMERICAN ACTOR

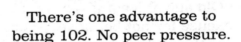

There's one advantage to
being 102. No peer pressure.

DENNIS WOLFBERG, AMERICAN COMEDIAN

Eighty's a landmark and people treat you differently than they do when you're 79. At 79, if you drop something it just lies there. At 80, people pick it up for you.

HELEN VAN SLYKE, WRITER

———•••———

The whiter my hair becomes, the more ready people are to believe what I say.

BERTRAND RUSSELL, BRITISH LOGICIAN AND PHILOSOPHER

———•••———

Old age at least gives me an excuse for not being very good at things that I was not very good at when I was young.

THOMAS SOWELL, AMERICAN WRITER

BIRTHDAYS

Birthdays are good
for you. Statistics
show that the people
who have the most
live the longest.

FATHER LARRY LORENZONI

A birthday is just the first day
of another 365-day journey
around the sun. Enjoy the trip.

ANONYMOUS

—•••—

When I turned two I was
really anxious, because I'd
doubled my age in a year. I
thought, if this keeps up, by
the time I'm six I'll be 90.

STEVEN WRIGHT, AMERICAN COMEDIAN, ACTOR AND WRITER

My wife hasn't had
a birthday in four
years. She was born
in the year of our
Lord-only-knows.

ANONYMOUS

You're getting old when the only
thing you want for your birthday
is not to be reminded of it.

FELIX SEVERN

———•●●•———

Age is only a number.

LEXI STARLING

———•●●•———

For all the advances in
medicine, there is still no cure
for the common birthday.

JOHN GLENN, AMERICAN ASTRONAUT AND POLITICIAN

ELDERLY MUSINGS

And in the end, it's
not the years in your
life that count. It's
the life in your years.

ABRAHAM LINCOLN, AMERICAN PRESIDENT

There are many mysteries in old age but the greatest, surely, is this: in those adverts for walk-in bathtubs, why doesn't all the water gush out when you get in?

ALAN COREN, BRITISH WRITER AND SATIRIST

About the only thing that comes to us without effort is old age.

GLORIA PITZER, AMERICAN COOKERY WRITER

When you win, you're an old pro. When you lose, you're an old man.

CHARLEY CONERLY, AMERICAN FOOTBALL PLAYER

Life's tragedy is that we get old
too soon and wise too late.

BENJAMIN FRANKLIN, AMERICAN DIPLOMAT,
POLITICIAN AND PRINTER

———— •●• ————

Nobody loves life like him
who is growing old.

SOPHOCLES, GREEK TRAGEDIAN

———— •●• ————

One should never make
one's debut in a scandal. One
should reserve that to give
interest to one's old age.

OSCAR WILDE, IRISH POET, NOVELIST AND DRAMATIST

Oft from shrivelled skin
comes useful counsel.

SAEMUND, ICELANDIC PRIEST AND SCHOLAR

———— •●• ————

Life is a moderately good play
with a badly written third act.

TRUMAN CAPOTE, AMERICAN WRITER AND PLAYWRIGHT

———— •●• ————

A lady of a certain age, which
means certainly aged.

LORD BYRON, ROMANTIC POET AND SATIRIST

Anyone can get old. All you have to do is live long enough.

GROUCHO MARX, AMERICAN COMEDIAN, ACTOR AND SINGER

———•—•—

It's true, some wines improve with age. But only if the grapes were good in the first place.

ABIGAIL VAN BUREN, PEN NAME OF AMERICAN COLUMNIST PAULINE PHILLIPS AND HER SUCCESSOR, DAUGHTER JEANNE PHILLIPS

———•—•—

Grandchildren don't make a man feel old; it's the knowledge that he's married to a grandmother.

G. NORMAN COLLIE

Wisdom doesn't necessarily
come with age. Sometimes age
just shows up all by itself.

TOM WILSON, AMERICAN ACTOR, WRITER AND COMEDIAN

●●●

May you live all the
days of your life.

JONATHAN SWIFT, ANGLO-IRISH WRITER AND SATIRIST

By the time I have money to burn,
my fire will have burnt out.

ANONYMOUS

———•●•———

Life can only be understood
backwards, but it must
be lived forwards.

SØREN KIERKEGAARD, DANISH PHILOSOPHER AND THEOLOGIAN

Resolve to be tender with the
young, compassionate with
the aged, sympathetic with
the striving, and tolerant
with the weak and the wrong.
Sometime in your life you
will have been all of these.

DR ROBERT H. GODDARD, AMERICAN ROCKET ENGINEER

Life is a funny thing
that happens to you on
the way to the grave.

QUENTIN CRISP, BRITISH WRITER

Growing old is like being increasingly penalised for a crime you haven't committed.

ANTHONY POWELL, BRITISH WRITER

———— ●●● ————

I go slower as time goes faster.

MASON COOLEY, AMERICAN APHORIST

Half our life is spent trying
to find something to do with
the time we have rushed
through life trying to save.

WILL ROGERS

———•●•———

Men who are orthodox when
they are young are in danger of
being middle-aged all their lives.

WALTER LIPPMANN, AMERICAN WRITER,
JOURNALIST AND POLITICAL COMMENTATOR

Old age is life's parody.

SIMONE DE BEAUVOIR, FRENCH WRITER AND PHILOSOPHER

———•●•———

When I was young, I thought
that money was the most
important thing in life; now
that I am old, I know it is.

OSCAR WILDE

———•●•———

Well enough for old folks to rise
early, because they have done
so many mean things all their
lives they can't sleep anyhow.

MARK TWAIN, AMERICAN WRITER

I am long on ideas, but
short on time.
I expect to live to be only
about a hundred.

THOMAS ALVA EDISON, AMERICAN
INVENTOR AND BUSINESSMAN

———●●●———

Age is something that doesn't
matter, unless you are a cheese.

BILLIE BURKE, AMERICAN ACTRESS

———●●●———

Old age is the verdict of life.

AMELIA E. BARR, ENGLISH-BORN AMERICAN
WRITER AND JOURNALIST

I don't believe one grows older.
I think that what happens early
on in life is that at a certain age
one stands still and stagnates.

T. S. ELIOT, AMERICAN-BORN BRITISH
PLAYWRIGHT, POET AND CRITIC

Growing old is something
you do if you're lucky.

GROUCHO MARX

Age wrinkles the body.
Quitting wrinkles the soul.

DOUGLAS MACARTHUR, AMERICAN GENERAL

You can't turn back
the clock. But you can
wind it up again.

BONNIE PRUDDEN, AMERICAN ROCK CLIMBER

EXPERIENCE, MISTAKES AND ADVICE

For the first half of your life, people tell you what you should do; for the second half, they tell you what you should have done.

RICHARD NEEDHAM

If I had my life to live over again, I'd be a plumber.

ALBERT EINSTEIN, GERMAN-SWISS-AMERICAN THEORETICAL PHYSICIST

———•●•———

I get to be a kid now, because I wasn't a kid when I was supposed to be one. But in some ways, I'm like an old woman – lived it, seen it, done it, been there, have the T-shirt.

DREW BARRYMORE, AMERICAN ACTRESS

———•●•———

If I had my life to live over again, I'd make the same mistakes, only sooner.

TALLULAH BANKHEAD, AMERICAN ACTRESS

Age is a high price to
pay for maturity.

TOM STOPPARD, BRITISH PLAYWRIGHT

———•••———

The man who views the world
at 50 the same as he did at 20
has wasted 30 years of his life.

MUHAMMAD ALI, AMERICAN BOXER

———•••———

My greatest regret is not
knowing at 30 what I knew
about women at 60.

ARTHUR MILLER, AMERICAN PLAYWRIGHT AND ESSAYIST

Whenever I get down about
life going by too quickly, what
helps me is a little mantra
that I repeat to myself: at
least I'm not a fruit fly.

RAY ROMANO, AMERICAN COMEDIAN AND ACTOR

I'll never make the mistake
of being 70 again.

CASEY STENGEL, AMERICAN BASEBALL PLAYER AND MANAGER

Autumn is mellower, and
what we lose in flowers, we
more than gain in fruits.

SAMUEL BUTLER, BRITISH WRITER AND CRITIC

I used to have a sign over my computer that read 'Old dogs can learn new tricks', but lately I sometimes ask myself how many more new tricks I want to learn. Wouldn't it just be easier to be outdated?

RAM DASS, AMERICAN PROFESSOR OF PSYCHOLOGY, RESEARCHER AND WRITER

A prune is an experienced plum.

JOHN TRATTNER, AMERICAN DIPLOMAT,
WRITER AND JOURNALIST

You don't appreciate a lot of stuff in school until you get older. Little things like being spanked every day by a middle-aged woman: stuff you pay good money for in later life.

EMO PHILIPS, AMERICAN COMEDIAN

We learn from experience that men never learn anything from experience.

GEORGE BERNARD SHAW, IRISH LITERARY CRITIC, PLAYWRIGHT
AND 1925 NOBEL PRIZE WINNER FOR LITERATURE

The post office has a great charm at one point of our lives. When you have lived to my age you will begin to think letters are never worth going through the rain for.

JANE AUSTEN, BRITISH NOVELIST AND WRITER

When I was young, I was told: 'You'll see when you're 50.' I'm 50 and I haven't seen a thing.

ERIK SATIE, FRENCH COMPOSER AND PIANIST

I have lived in the world just long enough to look carefully the second time into those things that I am most certain of the first time.

JOSH BILLINGS, AMERICAN WRITER AND LECTURER

I advise you to go on living solely to enrage those who are paying your annuities. It is the only pleasure I have left.

VOLTAIRE, FRENCH PHILOSOPHER AND WRITER

———•••———

Cherish all your happy moments: they make a fine cushion for old age.

CHRISTOPHER MORLEY, AMERICAN JOURNALIST, NOVELIST AND POET

———•••———

When people tell you how young you look, they are also telling you how old you are.

CARY GRANT, ENGLISH-BORN AMERICAN ACTOR

As I grow older, I pay less attention to what men say. I just watch what they do.

ANDREW CARNEGIE, SCOTTISH-BORN AMERICAN INDUSTRIALIST AND PHILANTHROPIST

———•●●———

Experience is a comb life gives you after you lose your hair.

JUDITH STERN, WRITER

———•●●———

The time to begin most things is ten years ago.

MIGNON MCLAUGHLIN, AMERICAN JOURNALIST AND AUTHOR

Just remember, once you're over the hill, you begin to pick up speed.

CHARLES M. SCHULZ, AMERICAN CARTOONIST

GROWING OLD GRACEFULLY

When it comes to staying young, a mind-lift beats a face-lift any day.

MARTY BUCELLA, CARTOONIST

The only real way to look younger
is not to be born so soon.

CHARLES M. SCHULZ

Age should not have its face
lifted, but it should rather teach
the world to admire wrinkles
as the etching of experience
and the firm line of character.

CLARENCE DAY, AMERICAN WRITER

Let us respect grey hairs,
especially our own.

J. P. SEARS

The best mirror is an old friend.

GEORGE HERBERT, BRITISH POET AND CLERGYMAN

———•●•———

Don't retouch my wrinkles in
the photograph. I would not
want it to be thought that I had
lived for all these years without
having anything to show for it.

QUEEN ELIZABETH, THE QUEEN MOTHER

———•●•———

I'd like to grow very old
as slowly as possible.

IRENE MAYER SELZNICK, AMERICAN THEATRICAL PRODUCER

How foolish to think that one
can ever slam the door in the
face of age. Much wiser to be
polite and gracious and ask
him to lunch in advance.

NOËL COWARD, BRITISH ACTOR, COMPOSER AND PLAYWRIGHT

———— •●• ————

A woman past 40 should
make up her mind to be
young, and not her face.

BILLIE BURKE

———— •●• ————

Time may be a great healer,
but it's a lousy beautician.

ANONYMOUS

I don't plan to grow old
gracefully; I plan to have
facelifts until my ears meet.

RITA RUDNER, AMERICAN WRITER AND COMEDIAN

———•●•———

The easiest way to diminish
the appearance of wrinkles
is to keep your glasses off
when you look in the mirror.

JOAN RIVERS, AMERICAN COMEDIAN

———•●•———

Beautiful young people
are accidents of nature,
but beautiful old people
are works of art.

ELEANOR ROOSEVELT, FIRST LADY OF THE UNITED STATES

GRUMPINESS

There is absolutely
nothing to be said
in favour of growing
old. There ought to be
legislation against it.

PATRICK MOORE

The older a man gets, the farther
he had to walk to school as a boy.

HENRY BRIGHTMAN

———•●•———

The older you get the
stronger the wind gets – and
it's always in your face.

JACK NICKLAUS, AMERICAN GOLFER

———•●•———

I refused to go on that *Grumpy
Old Men* programme because I
said, 'If I go on, I will be grumpy
about grumpy old men.'

STEPHEN FRY, BRITISH COMEDIAN, ACTOR AND WRITER

Some grow bitter with age;
the more their teeth drop out,
the more biting they get.

GEORGE D. PRENTICE, AMERICAN
NEWSPAPER EDITOR AND WRITER

———•●•———

There's no law that decrees
when not to whinge, but
you reach a certain age – 80
seems about right – when
you're expected to manifest
querulousness – the coffee's too
hot, the boiled egg's too soft...

CLEMENT FREUD, BRITISH WRITER,
BROADCASTER AND POLITICIAN

My Uncle Sammy was an angry man. He had printed on his tombstone: What are you looking at?

MARGARET SMITH, AMERICAN COMEDIAN

—•●•—

If old people were to mobilise en masse they would constitute a formidable fighting force, as anyone who has ever had the temerity to try to board a bus ahead of a little old lady with an umbrella well knows.

VERA FORRESTER

HEALTH AND EXERCISE

I am getting to an age
when I can only enjoy
the last sport left.
It is called hunting
for your spectacles.

SIR EDWARD GREY, POLITICIAN AND ORNITHOLOGIST

At my age getting a second doctor's opinion is kinda like switching slot machines.

JIMMY CARTER, AMERICAN PRESIDENT

———•••———

To win back my youth...
there is nothing I wouldn't
do – except take exercise,
get up early, or be a useful
member of the community.

OSCAR WILDE

———•••———

The denunciation of the young is a necessary part of the hygiene of older people, and greatly assists in the circulation of their blood.

LOGAN PEARSALL SMITH, AMERICAN ESSAYIST AND CRITIC

People who say you're just
as old as you feel are all
wrong, fortunately.

RUSSELL BAKER, AMERICAN WRITER

———•●•———

I'd like to learn to ski but I'm 44
and I'm worried about my knees.
They creak a lot and I'm afraid
they might start an avalanche.

JONATHAN ROSS, BRITISH COMEDIAN AND
TELEVISION AND RADIO PRESENTER

———•●•———

My mother is no spring chicken
although she has got as many
chemicals in her as one.

DAME EDNA EVERAGE, ALTER EGO OF AUSTRALIAN
COMEDIAN BARRY HUMPHRIES

If I'm feeling really
wild I don't floss
before bedtime.

JUDITH VIORST, AMERICAN WRITER

Exercise daily. Eat wisely.
Die anyway.

ANONYMOUS

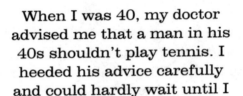

When I was 40, my doctor
advised me that a man in his
40s shouldn't play tennis. I
heeded his advice carefully
and could hardly wait until I
reached 50 to start again.

HUGO L. BLACK, AMERICAN JURIST, LAWYER AND POLITICIAN

Old people should not eat
health foods. They need all the
preservatives they can get.

ROBERT ORBEN, AMERICAN MAGICIAN AND COMEDY WRITER

I've just become a pensioner
so I've started saving up for
my own hospital trolley.

TOM BAKER, BRITISH ACTOR

———•●•———

If, at the age of 30, you are stiff
and out of shape, then you are
old. If, at 60, you are supple and
strong, then you are young.

JOSEPH PILATES, GREEK-GERMAN INVENTOR OF PILATES

———•●•———

Middle age is when you
are not inclined to exercise
anything but caution.

ARTHUR MURRAY, AMERICAN DANCE
INSTRUCTOR AND BUSINESSMAN

Each year it grows
harder to make ends
meet – the ends I refer
to are hands and feet.

RICHARD ARMOUR, AMERICAN POET AND AUTHOR

If you rest, you rust.

HELEN HAYES, AMERICAN STAGE AND FILM ACTRESS

———•••———

You can't be as old as I am without waking up with a surprised look on your face every morning, 'Holy Christ, what da ya know – I'm still around!' It's absolutely amazing that I survived all the booze and smoking and the cars and the career.

PAUL NEWMAN, AMERICAN ACTOR

———•••———

As for me, except for an occasional heart attack, I feel as young as I ever did.

ROBERT BENCHLEY, AMERICAN ACTOR AND WRITER

I don't want a flu jab. I like
getting flu. It gives me something
else to complain about.

DAVID LETTERMAN, AMERICAN TELEVISION TALK SHOW HOST

———— •●• ————

One of the advantages of being
70 is that you need only four
hours' sleep. True, you need
it four times a day, but still.

DENIS NORDEN, BRITISH COMEDY WRITER
AND TELEVISION PRESENTER

———— •●• ————

I keep fit. Every morning,
I do a hundred laps of an
Olympic-sized swimming pool
– in a small motor launch.

PETER COOK, BRITISH ACTOR AND COMEDIAN

I guess I don't so much mind being old, as I mind being fat and old.

PETER GABRIEL, ENGLISH MUSICIAN

When you get to my age life
seems little more than one long
march to and from the lavatory.

JOHN MORTIMER, BRITISH WRITER

Now I'm getting older I take
health supplements: geranium,
dandelion, passionflower,
hibiscus. I feel great, and
when I pee, I experience the
fresh scent of potpourri.

SHEILA WENZ, AMERICAN COMEDIAN

Now I'm over 50 my doctor
says I should go out and get
more fresh air and exercise.
I said, 'All right, I'll drive
with the car window open.'

ANGUS WALKER

HOW OLD?

I do wish I could tell you my age but it's impossible. It keeps changing all the time.

GREER GARSON, BRITISH ACTRESS

Old age is always 15 years
older than what I am.

BERNARD BARUCH, AMERICAN ECONOMIST
AND ADVISER TO AMERICAN PRESIDENTS

———•••———

The older I get, the older old is.

TOM BAKER

———•••———

I believe in loyalty; I think when
a woman reaches an age she
likes she should stick to it.

EVA GABOR, HUNGARIAN-BORN AMERICAN
ACTRESS AND ENTERTAINER

I'm 60 years of age.
That's 16 Celsius.

GEORGE CARLIN, AMERICAN STAND-UP
COMEDIAN, ACTOR AND WRITER

I am just turning 40 and
taking my time about it.

HAROLD LLOYD, AMERICAN ACTOR AND
FILM-MAKER, ON TURNING 77

I was born in 1962. True. And
the room next to me was 1963.

JOAN RIVERS

I refuse to admit that I am more
than 52, even if that makes
my children illegitimate.

NANCY ASTOR, AMERICAN-BORN POLITICIAN AND FIRST
WOMAN TO SIT IN THE BRITISH HOUSE OF COMMONS

●●●

No woman should ever
be quite accurate about her
age. It looks so calculating.

OSCAR WILDE

●●●

I'm not 40, I'm 18 with
22 years' experience.

ANONYMOUS

How Old?

Professionally, I have no age.

KATHLEEN TURNER, AMERICAN ACTRESS

———•••———

We're obsessed with age. Numbers are always and pointlessly attached to every name that's published in a newspaper: 'Joe Creamer, 43, and his daughter, Tiffany-Ann, 9, were merrily chasing a bunny, 2, when Tiffany-Ann tripped on the root of a tree, 106.'

JOAN RIVERS

———•••———

She may very well pass for 43 in the dusk with the light behind her!

W. S. GILBERT, BRITISH DRAMATIST AND LIBRETTIST

I don't know how old I am
because the goat ate the Bible
that had my birth certificate in
it. The goat lived to be 27.

SATCHEL PAIGE

• • •

I still think of myself as I
was 25 years ago. Then I look
in the mirror and see an old
bastard and I realise it's me.

DAVE ALLEN, IRISH COMEDIAN

• • •

First women subtract from their
age, then they divide it, and then
they extract its square root.

ANONYMOUS

Whenever the talk turns to
age, I say I am 49 plus VAT.

LIONEL BLAIR, BRITISH DANCER AND TELEVISION PRESENTER

* * *

I'm 65 and I guess that puts
me in with the geriatrics. But if
there were 15 months in every
year, I'd only be 48. That's the
trouble with us. We number
everything. Take women, for
example. I think they deserve
to have more than 12 years
between the ages of 28 and 40.

JAMES THURBER, AMERICAN WRITER AND CARTOONIST

* * *

Age is a number –
mine is unlisted.

ANONYMOUS

IMMORTALITY

Millions long for immortality who do not know what to do with themselves on a rainy Sunday afternoon.

He had decided to live forever
or die in the attempt.

JOSEPH HELLER, AMERICAN WRITER

———•●●———

The first step to eternal
life is you have to die.

CHUCK PALAHNIUK, AMERICAN JOURNALIST

———•●●———

There's nothing wrong with you
that reincarnation won't cure.

JACK E. LEONARD, AMERICAN COMEDIAN

The only thing wrong
with immortality is that it
tends to go on forever.

HERB CAEN, AMERICAN JOURNALIST

———•●•———

If you live to be 100, you've
got it made. Very few
people die past that age.

GEORGE BURNS, AMERICAN COMEDIAN AND ACTOR

———•●•———

I intend to live forever.
So far, so good.

STEVEN WRIGHT, AMERICAN COMEDIAN

MEMORY LOSS

As you get older
three things happen.
The first is your
memory goes, and
I can't remember
the other two...

NORMAN WISDOM, BRITISH COMEDIAN AND ACTOR

I believe the true function
of age is memory. I'm
recording as fast as I can.

RITA MAE BROWN, AMERICAN WRITER AND SOCIAL ACTIVIST

—— •●• ——

Once you've accumulated
sufficient knowledge to get by,
you're too old to remember it.

ANONYMOUS

—— •●• ——

They will all have heard that
story of yours before – but
if you tell it well they won't
mind hearing it again.

THORA HIRD, BRITISH ACTRESS

After the age of 80, everything
reminds you of something else.

LOWELL THOMAS, AMERICAN WRITER,
BROADCASTER AND TRAVELLER

———— •●• ————

Interviewer: 'Can you remember
any of your past lives?'
The Dalai Lama: 'At my age I
have a problem remembering
what happened yesterday.'

———— •●• ————

By the time you're 80 years
old you've learned everything.
You only have to remember it.

GEORGE BURNS

MIDDLE AGE

Middle age is the awkward period when Father Time starts catching up with Mother Nature.

HAROLD COFFIN, AMERICAN JOURNALIST

The really frightening thing about
middle age is the knowledge
that you'll grow out of it.

DORIS DAY, AMERICAN ACTRESS AND SINGER

———●●●———

It's hard to feel middle-aged,
because how can you tell how
long you are going to live?

MIGNON MCLAUGHLIN

———●●●———

Middle age is when your
broad mind and narrow waist
begin to change places.

E. JOSEPH COSSMAN, AMERICAN ENTREPRENEUR

Middle age is when you're old
enough to know better but
still young enough to do it.

OGDEN NASH

— •●• —

Middle age is when work
is a lot less fun, and fun
is a lot more work.

MILTON BERLE, AMERICAN COMEDIAN AND ACTOR

— •●• —

Years ago we discovered the
exact point, the dead centre of
middle age. It occurs when you
are too young to take up golf
and too old to rush to the net.

FRANKLIN ADAMS, AMERICAN JOURNALIST,
COLUMNIST AND TRANSLATOR

Middle age is the time when a man
is always thinking that in a week
or two he will feel as good as ever.

DON MARQUIS, AMERICAN COLUMNIST,
NOVELIST, PLAYWRIGHT AND POET

Setting a good example for
your children takes all the
fun out of middle age.

WILLIAM FEATHER, AMERICAN WRITER AND PUBLISHER

Middle age: When you
begin to exchange your
emotions for symptoms.

GEORGES CLÉMENCEAU, FRENCH DOCTOR AND JOURNALIST

Middle age is the time
in life when, after
pulling in your stomach,
you look as if you ought
to pull in your stomach.

ANONYMOUS

Middle age is when it takes
you all night to do once what
once you used to do all night.

KENNY EVERETT, BRITISH RADIO DJ AND TELEVISION ENTERTAINER

———•••———

Middle age is when
everything new you feel is
likely to be a symptom.

DR LAURENCE J. PETER, CANADIAN EDUCATOR

———•••———

Spiritual sloth, or acedia,
was known as The Sin of
the Middle Ages. It's the sin
of my middle age, too.

MIGNON MCLAUGHLIN

The long, dull, monotonous years
of middle-aged prosperity or
middle-aged adversity are excellent
campaigning weather for the devil.

C. S. LEWIS

—•●•—

You know you've reached middle
age when your weightlifting
consists merely of standing up.

BOB HOPE, ENGLISH-BORN AMERICAN ACTOR AND COMEDIAN

—•●•—

Middle age is when you're faced
with two temptations and you
choose the one that will get
you home by nine o'clock.

RONALD REAGAN, AMERICAN PRESIDENT

Middle age is when
you're sitting at home
on a Saturday night and
the telephone rings and
you hope it isn't for you.

OGDEN NASH

Mid-life crisis is that moment when
you realise your children and your
clothes are about the same age.

WILLIAM D. TAMMEUS, AMERICAN COLUMNIST

Middle age is when
your age starts to show
around your middle.

BOB HOPE

Middle age – later than
you think and sooner
than you expect.

EARL WILSON, BASEBALL PLAYER

NATURE OF OLD AGE

The first 40 years of
life give us the text:
the next 30 supply
the commentary.

ARTHUR SCHOPENHAUER, GERMAN PHILOSOPHER

As we grow older, our bodies get shorter and our anecdotes longer.

ROBERT QUILLEN, AMERICAN HUMORIST, JOURNALIST AND CARTOONIST

———— •●• ————

You know you've grown up when you become obsessed with the thermostat.

JEFF FOXWORTHY, AMERICAN COMEDIAN AND ACTOR

———— •●• ————

As one grows older, one becomes wiser and more foolish.

FRANÇOIS DE LA ROCHEFOUCAULD, CLASSICAL WRITER, LEADING EXPONENT OF THE MAXIME

An old man looks permanent, as
if he had been born an old man.

H. E. BATES, BRITISH WRITER

•••

The essence of age is
intellect. Wherever that
appears, we call it old.

RALPH WALDO EMERSON

•••

Time and trouble will
tame an advanced young
woman, but an advanced old
woman is uncontrollable
by any earthly force.

DOROTHY L. SAYERS, BRITISH WRITER

Old age means realising
you will never own all
the dogs you wanted to.

JOE GORES, AMERICAN WRITER

Forty is the old age of youth;
50 is the youth of old age.

FRENCH PROVERB

Growing old is no more than
a bad habit, which a busy
person has no time to form.

ANDRE MAUROIS, FRENCH BIOGRAPHER, NOVELIST AND ESSAYIST

Age seldom arrives smoothly
or quickly. It's more often
a succession of jerks.

JEAN RHYS, DOMINICAN NOVELIST

NOT GROWING UP

It takes a long time
to grow young.

PABLO PICASSO

Life would be infinitely happier if
we could only be born at the age
of 80 and gradually approach 18.

MARK TWAIN

Age does not diminish the
extreme disappointment
of having a scoop of ice
cream fall from the cone.

JIM FIEBIG

The surprising thing about
young fools is how many
survive to become old fools.

DOUG LARSON, AMERICAN COLUMNIST

The older you get the more
important it is not to act your age.

ASHLEIGH BRILLIANT, BRITISH-BORN
AMERICAN WRITER AND CARTOONIST

Growing old is compulsory,
growing up is optional.

BOB MONKHOUSE, BRITISH COMEDIAN

You're only young once, but
you can be immature forever.

GERMAINE GREER, AUSTRALIAN ACADEMIC AND JOURNALIST

The secret of genius is to carry
the spirit of the child into
old age, which means never
losing your enthusiasm.

ALDOUS HUXLEY, BRITISH WRITER

⎯⎯⎯⎯•●●•⎯⎯⎯⎯

I plan on growing old much
later in life, or maybe not at all.

PATTY CAREY

⎯⎯⎯⎯•●●•⎯⎯⎯⎯

Almost all my middle-aged
and elderly acquaintances,
including me, feel about 25,
unless we haven't had our coffee,
in which case we feel 107.

MARTHA BECK, AMERICAN SOCIOLOGIST AND WRITER

The tragedy of old age is not that
one is old, but that one is young.

OSCAR WILDE

———•••———

I've got to go and see the old folk.

QUEEN ELIZABETH, THE QUEEN MOTHER AT AGE 97, SPOTTING
A GROUP OF PENSIONERS AT CHELTENHAM RACECOURSE

———•••———

Inside every older person is
a younger person wondering
what the hell happened.

CORA HARVEY ARMSTRONG

When they tell me
I'm too old to do
something, I attempt
it immediately.

PABLO PICASSO

PLEASURES OF OLD AGE

My grandmother
is over 80 and still
doesn't need glasses.
Drinks right out
of the bottle.

HENRY YOUNGMAN, ENGLISH-BORN AMERICAN
COMEDIAN AND VIOLINIST

You know you're getting old
when a four-letter word for
something pleasurable two
people can do in bed is R-E-A-D.

DENIS NORDEN

* ● ● *

One of the many pleasures of
old age is giving things up.

MALCOLM MUGGERIDGE, BRITISH JOURNALIST AND AUTHOR

* ● ● *

I smoke 10 to 15 cigars a
day, at my age I have to
hold on to something.

GEORGE BURNS

Jameson's Irish Whiskey really
does improve with age: the
older I get the more I like it.

BOB MONKHOUSE

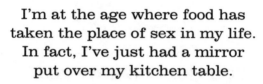

I'm at the age where food has
taken the place of sex in my life.
In fact, I've just had a mirror
put over my kitchen table.

RODNEY DANGERFIELD, AMERICAN COMEDIAN AND ACTOR

I always make a point of
starting the day at 6 a.m. with
champagne. It goes straight
to the heart and cheers one
up. White wine won't do.
You need the bubbles.

JOHN MORTIMER

PHYSICAL EFFECTS

You don't know real
embarrassment until
your hip sets off a
metal detector.

ROSS MCGUINNESS

You know you're getting old when everything hurts. And what doesn't hurt doesn't work.

HY GARDNER, AMERICAN COLUMNIST

———•••———

Have you not a moist eye, a dry hand, a yellow cheek, a white beard, a decreasing leg, an increasing belly? Is not your voice broken, your wind short, your chin double, your wit single, and every part about you blasted with antiquity?

WILLIAM SHAKESPEARE, ENGLISH POET AND PLAYWRIGHT

———•••———

I have the body of an 18 year-old. I keep it in the fridge.

SPIKE MILLIGAN, IRISH COMEDIAN

I don't want to end up in an old
folk's home wearing incompetence
pads. I'm still compost mentis.

HARRIET WYNN

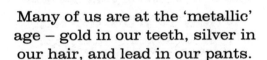

Many of us are at the 'metallic'
age – gold in our teeth, silver in
our hair, and lead in our pants.

ANONYMOUS

Advanced old age is when
you sit in a rocking chair
and can't get it going.

ELIAKIM KATZ, CANADIAN PROFESSOR OF ECONOMICS

I knew I was going bald
when it was taking
longer and longer
to wash my face.

HARRY HILL, BRITISH COMEDIAN

They say that age is all in your mind. The trick is keeping it from creeping down into your body.

ANONYMOUS

———•●●•———

I don't need you to remind me of my age, I have a bladder to do that for me.

STEPHEN FRY

———•●●•———

Life begins at 40 – but so do fallen arches, rheumatism, faulty eyesight, and the tendency to tell a story to the same person three or four times.

HELEN ROWLAND, ENGLISH-AMERICAN WRITER

It's been said that if you're not
radical at 20, you have no heart; if
you're still radical at 40, you have
no brain. Of course, either way,
at 60 you usually have no teeth.

BILL MAHER, AMERICAN COMEDIAN,
ACTOR, WRITER AND PRODUCER

———— ●●● ————

Everything slows down with age,
except the time it takes cake and
ice cream to reach your hips.

JOHN WAGNER

———— ●●● ————

I don't feel 80. In fact I don't
feel anything until noon,
then it's time for my nap.

BOB HOPE

They talk about the economy
this year. Hey, my hairline
is in recession, my waistline
is in inflation. Altogether,
I'm in a depression.

RICK MAJERUS

It's extraordinary. My
mother doesn't need glasses
at all and here I am at 52,
56 – well, whatever age I am
– and can't see a thing.

QUEEN ELIZABETH II

Wrinkles should merely indicate
where smiles have been.

MARK TWAIN

Thoughtfulness begets wrinkles.

CHARLES DICKENS, BRITISH NOVELIST

———•••———

My grandma told me, 'The good news is, after menopause the hair on your legs gets really thin and you don't have to shave any more. Which is great because it means you have more time to work on your new moustache.'

KAREN HABER, AMERICAN WRITER

———•••———

Robert Redford used to be such a handsome man and now look at him: everything has dropped, expanded and turned a funny colour.

GEORGE BEST, IRISH FOOTBALL PLAYER

After a certain number of years
our faces become our biographies.

CYNTHIA OZICK, AMERICAN WRITER

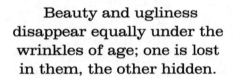

Beauty and ugliness
disappear equally under the
wrinkles of age; one is lost
in them, the other hidden.

JEAN ANTOINE PETIT-SENN, FRENCH-SWISS POET

Like a lot of fellows around here,
I have a furniture problem. My
chest has fallen into my drawers.

BILLY CASPER, AMERICAN GOLFER

Grey hair is God's graffiti.

BILL COSBY, AMERICAN ACTOR, COMEDIAN AND PRODUCER

———•••———

At 75, I sleep like a log. I never
have to get up in the middle of
the night to go to the bathroom.
I go in the morning. Every
morning, like clockwork, at
7 a.m., I pee. Unfortunately,
I don't wake up till 8.

HARRY BECKWORTH

———•••———

I used to think I'd like less grey
hair. Now I'd like more of it.

RICHIE BENAUD, AUSTRALIAN CRICKETER

Alas, after a certain age every man is responsible for his face.

ALBERT CAMUS, FRENCH NOVELIST, ESSAYIST AND PLAYWRIGHT

I'm at an age where my back goes out more than I do.

PHYLLIS DILLER, AMERICAN COMEDIAN

I had a job selling hearing aids from door to door. It wasn't easy, because your best prospects never answered.

BOB MONKHOUSE

RETIREMENT

People ought to retire at 40 when they feel over-used and go back to work at 65 when they feel useless.

SISTER CAROL ANNE O'MARIE, AMERICAN NUN AND WRITER

Retired is being tired twice... first tired of working, then tired of not.

RICHARD ARMOUR

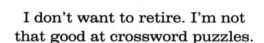

I don't want to retire. I'm not that good at crossword puzzles.

NORMAN MAILER, AMERICAN WRITER

My parents live in a retirement community, which is basically a minimum-security prison with a golf course.

JOEL WARSHAW

When a man falls into his anecdotage, it is a sign for him to retire from the world.

BENJAMIN DISRAELI, 1ST EARL OF BEACONSFIELD AND BRITISH PRIME MINISTER

• ● •

Don't retire, retread!

ROBERT OTTERBOURG, AMERICAN WRITER

• ● •

We spend our lives on the run: we get up by the clock, eat and sleep by the clock, get up again, go to work – and then we retire. And what do they give us? A bloody clock.

DAVE ALLEN

The best time to start thinking
about your retirement is
before the boss does.

ANONYMOUS

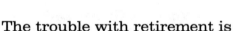

The trouble with retirement is
that you never get a day off.

ABE LEMONS, BASKETBALL COACH

Once it was impossible to
find any Bond villains older
than myself, I retired.

ROGER MOORE, BRITISH ACTOR

SECRETS OF LONGEVITY

You can live to be a
hundred if you give
up all the things that
make you want to
live to be a hundred.

WOODY ALLEN

Old age is no place for sissies.

BETTE DAVIS, AMERICAN ACTRESS

———●●●———

Interviewer: 'You've reached the ripe old age of 121. What do you expect the future will be like?' Jeanne Calment: 'Very short.'

———●●●———

Every one desires to live long, but no one would be old.

JONATHAN SWIFT

My first advice on how not to grow old would be to choose your ancestors carefully.

BERTRAND RUSSELL

— •●• —

The fountain of youth is a mixture of gin and vermouth.

COLE PORTER, AMERICAN COMPOSER AND SONGWRITER

Old age is like everything else. To make a success of it, you've got to start young.

THEODORE ROOSEVELT, AMERICAN PRESIDENT

———•●•———

I've found a formula for avoiding these exaggerated fears of age; you take care of every day – let the calendar take care of the years.

ED WYNN, AMERICAN ACTOR

The great secret that all old people share is that you really haven't changed in 70 or 80 years. Your body changes, but you don't change at all. And that, of course, causes great confusion.

DORIS LESSING, BRITISH WRITER

• • •

More people would live to a ripe old age if they weren't too busy providing for it.

ANONYMOUS

It's a good idea to obey all the rules when you're young just so you'll have the strength to break them when you're old.

MARK TWAIN

— ●●● —

A man 90 years old was asked to what he attributed his longevity. I reckon, he said, with a twinkle in his eye, it's because most nights I went to bed and slept when I should have sat up and worried.

DOROTHEA KENT, AMERICAN ACTRESS

Ageing seems to be the only
available way to live a long life.

DANIEL AUBER, FRENCH COMPOSER

———•••———

The idea is to die young
as late as possible.

ASHLEY MONTAGU, BRITISH ANTHROPOLOGIST AND HUMANIST

———•••———

I'll tell ya how to stay young:
hang around with older people.

BOB HOPE

A man's only as old as
the woman he feels.

GROUCHO MARX

Age is a question of mind
over matter. If you don't
mind, it doesn't matter!

MARK TWAIN

• • •

Since people are going to
be living longer and getting
older, they'll just have to learn
how to be babies longer.

ANDY WARHOL, AMERICAN ARTIST

I can only assume that it is
largely due to the accumulation
of toasts to my health over the
years that I am still enjoying
a fairly satisfactory state of
health and have reached such
an unexpectedly great age.

PRINCE PHILIP, THE DUKE OF EDINBURGH

•••

The secret of staying young
is to live honestly, eat slowly
and lie about your age.

LUCILLE BALL, AMERICAN ACTRESS AND COMEDIAN

To stop ageing –
keep on raging.

MICHAEL FORBES, AMERICAN POLITICIAN

SENILITY

They tell you that
you'll lose your mind
when you grow older.
What they don't tell
you is that you won't
miss it very much.

MALCOLM COWLEY, AMERICAN CRITIC, WRITER
AND EDITOR OF *THE NEW REPUBLIC*

I am in the prime of senility.

BENJAMIN FRANKLIN

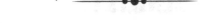

When I was young I was called a
rugged individualist. When I was
in my fifties I was considered
eccentric. Here I am doing and
saying the same things I did
then and I'm labelled senile.

GEORGE BURNS

When you become senile,
you won't know it.

BILL COSBY

How the hell should I know?
Most of the people my age are
dead. You could look it up.

CASEY STENGEL

●●●

They say that after the age
of 20 you lose 50,000 brain
cells a day. I don't believe
it. I think it's much more.

NED SHERRIN, BRITISH BROADCASTER,
WRITER AND STAGE DIRECTOR

●●●

My experience is that as soon
as people are old enough
to know better, they don't
know anything at all.

OSCAR WILDE

SEX AND INDECENCY

Old age is an excellent
time for outrage. My
goal is to say or do at
least one outrageous
thing every week.

MAGGIE KUHN

Sex manual for the
more mature – 'How
to tell an orgasm from
a heart attack!'

ANONYMOUS

A medical report states that
the human male is physically
capable of enjoying sex up to and
even beyond the age of 80. Not
as a participant, of course...

DENIS NORDEN

———•••———

Don't worry about temptation
as you grow older, it
starts avoiding you.

WINSTON CHURCHILL, BRITISH PRIME MINISTER

———•••———

The older one grows, the
more one likes indecency.

VIRGINIA WOOLF, BRITISH WRITER

I've always thought that the
stereotype of the dirty old
man is really the creation
of a dirty young man who
wants the field to himself.

HUGH DOWNS, AMERICAN TELEVISION
HOST, PRODUCER AND WRITER

———•●•———

No matter. The dead bird
does not fall out of the nest.

WINSTON CHURCHILL ON BEING TOLD HIS FLIES WERE UNDONE

———•●•———

Middle age is when a guy
keeps turning off the lights
for economical rather
then romantic reasons.

LILLIAN CARTER

After a man passes 60, his mischief is mainly in his head.

EDGAR WATSON HOWE, AMERICAN EDITOR AND WRITER

What most persons consider
as virtue, after the age of 40
is simply a loss of energy.

VOLTAIRE

Now that I'm 78, I do Tantric
sex because it's very slow. My
favourite position is called
the plumber. You stay in all
day but nobody comes.

JOHN MORTIMER

Talk about getting old. I was
getting dressed and a peeping
tom looked in the window, took a
look and pulled down the shade.

JOAN RIVERS

Old age likes indecency.
It's a sign of life.

MASON COOLEY

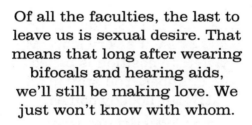

Of all the faculties, the last to
leave us is sexual desire. That
means that long after wearing
bifocals and hearing aids,
we'll still be making love. We
just won't know with whom.

JACK PAAR, AMERICAN RADIO AND
TELEVISION TALK SHOW HOST

I can still enjoy sex at 75. I
live at 76, so it's no distance.

BOB MONKHOUSE

SIGNS OF OLD AGE

They say the first
thing to go when
you're old is your
legs or your eyesight.
It isn't true. The
first thing to go is
parallel parking.

KURT VONNEGUT, AMERICAN NOVELIST,
SATIRIST AND GRAPHIC ARTIST

You know you're old if they have
discontinued your blood type.

PHYLLIS DILLER

———•●•———

It's a sign of age if you
feel like the morning after
the night before and you
haven't been anywhere.

ANONYMOUS

———•●•———

You're an old-timer if
you can remember when
setting the world on fire
was a figure of speech.

FRANKLIN P. JONES, AMERICAN BUSINESSMAN

Old age is when the liver spots
show through your gloves.

PHYLLIS DILLER

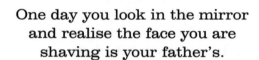

One day you look in the mirror
and realise the face you are
shaving is your father's.

ROBERT HARRIS, BRITISH WRITER

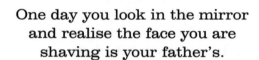

One of the signs of old age
is that you have to carry
your senses around in your
handbag – glasses, hearing
aids, dentures etc.

KURT STRAUSS, AMERICAN ACTOR AND VOICE ACTOR

You know you are getting
old when the candles cost
more than the cake.

BOB HOPE

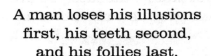

A man loses his illusions
first, his teeth second,
and his follies last.

HELEN ROWLAND

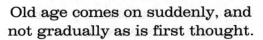

Old age comes on suddenly, and
not gradually as is first thought.

EMILY DICKINSON, AMERICAN POET

There is only one cure for grey.
It was invented by a Frenchman.
It is called the guillotine.

P. G. WODEHOUSE, BRITISH WRITER

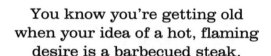

You know you're getting old
when your idea of a hot, flaming
desire is a barbecued steak.

VICTORIA FABIANO

You know you're getting older
when the first thing you do
after you're done eating is
look for a place to lie down.

LOUIE ANDERSON, AMERICAN COMEDIAN, WRITER AND ACTOR

Inflation is when you pay
fifteen dollars for the ten-dollar
haircut you used to get for five
dollars when you had hair.

SAM EWING, AMERICAN WRITER

———•••———

The first sign of maturity is
the discovery that the volume
knob also turns to the left.

JERRY M. WRIGHT

———•••———

First, you forget names, then you
forget faces. Next, you forget to
pull your zipper up and finally
you forget to pull it down.

LEO ROSENBERG

You know you're getting old
when all the names in your black
book have M.D. after them.

ARNOLD PALMER, AMERICAN GOLFER

———— •●• ————

You know you're getting
older if you have more
fingers than real teeth.

RODNEY DANGERFIELD

STYLE

If you really want
to annoy your
glamorous, well-
preserved 42-year-
old auntie, say, 'I bet
you were really pretty
when you were young.'

LILY SAVAGE, ALTER EGO OF BRITISH COMEDIAN
AND TELEVISION PRESENTER PAUL O'GRADY

Age becomes reality when you hear someone refer to 'that attractive young woman standing next to the woman in the green dress', and you find that you're the one in the green dress.

LOIS WYSE, AMERICAN WRITER

———•••———

You know you're getting old when you're dashing through Marks and Spencer's, spot a pair of Dr Scholl's sandals, stop, and think, *hmm, they look comfy.*

VICTORIA WOOD, BRITISH COMEDIAN, ACTRESS AND WRITER

———•••———

My dad's pants kept creeping up on him. By 65 he was just a pair of pants and a head.

JEFF ALTMAN, AMERICAN COMEDIAN

TALKING 'BOUT THE GENERATIONS

It's hard for me to get used to these changing times. I can remember when the air was clean and sex was dirty.

GEORGE BURNS

My generation thought 'fast food' was something you ate during Lent, a 'Big Mac' was an oversized raincoat and 'crumpet' was something you had for tea. 'Sheltered accommodation' was a place where you waited for a bus, 'time-sharing' meant togetherness and you kept 'coke' in the coal house.

JOAN COLLINS, BRITISH ACTRESS

At the age of 20, we don't care what the world thinks of us; at 30 we worry about what it is thinking of us; at 40, we discover that it wasn't thinking of us at all.

ANONYMOUS

There are three periods in life: youth, middle age and 'how well you look'.

NELSON ROCKEFELLER, AMERICAN VICE PRESIDENT AND GOVERNOR OF NEW YORK

———●●———

Girls used to come up to me and say, 'My sister loves you.' Now girls come up to me and say, 'My mother loves you.'

LEE MAZZILLI, AMERICAN BASEBALL PLAYER

———●●———

Youth is the time of getting, middle age of improving, and old age of spending.

ANNE BRADSTREET, AMERICAN POET

Parents often talk about the
younger generation as if they
didn't have anything to do with it.

DR HAIM GINOTT, PSYCHOLOGIST AND WRITER

———•●•———

At 16 I was stupid, confused
and indecisive. At 25 I was wise,
self-confident, prepossessing
and assertive. At 45 I am
stupid, confused, insecure and
indecisive. Who would have
supposed that maturity is only
a short break in adolescence?

JULES FEIFFER, AMERICAN CARTOONIST AND WRITER

Wrinkles are hereditary. Parents get them from their children.

DORIS DAY

Why do grandparents and grandchildren get along so well? They have the same enemy – the mother.

CLAUDETTE COLBERT, FRENCH-BORN AMERICAN ACTRESS

When you are about 35 years old, something terrible always happens to music.

STEVE RACE, BRITISH PIANIST, COMPOSER AND RADIO DISC JOCKEY

There are three stages in an actor's career: Who is John Amos? Get me John Amos. Get me a young John Amos.

JOHN AMOS, AMERICAN ACTOR

———◆●◆———

My nan said, 'What do you mean when you say the computer went down on you?'

JOSEPH LONGTHORNE

———◆●◆———

There are three stages of man: he believes in Santa Claus; he does not believe in Santa Claus; he is Santa Claus.

BOB PHILLIPS, AMERICAN WRITER

At 20 years of age the will reigns;
at 30 the wit; at 40 the judgement.

BENJAMIN FRANKLIN

———•●•———

In case you're worried about
what's going to become of the
younger generation, it's going
to grow up and start worrying
about the younger generation.

ROGER ALLEN, AMERICAN WRITER

———•●•———

No matter how old a
mother is she watches her
middle-aged children for
signs of improvement.

FLORIDA SCOTT MAXWELL, AMERICAN
WRITER AND PLAYWRIGHT

The children despise their parents
until the age of 40, when they
suddenly become just like them
– thus preserving the system.

QUENTIN CREWE, BRITISH WRITER

———————•●•———————

Be kind to your kids, they'll be
choosing your nursing home.

ANONYMOUS

———————•●•———————

The first half of our life is
ruined by our parents – and the
second half by our children.

CLARENCE DARROW, AMERICAN LAWYER, SPEAKER AND WRITER

THOUGHTS ON DEATH AND THE AFTERLIFE

Since I got to 80, I've started reading the Bible a lot more. It's kind of like cramming for my finals.

VINCENT WATSON

I used to hate weddings – all those old dears poking me in the stomach and saying 'You're next'. But they stopped all that when I started doing the same to them at funerals.

GAIL FLYNN

———•●●•———

There are worse things in life than death. Have you ever spent an evening with an insurance salesman?

WOODY ALLEN

I want to die young at
an advanced age.

MAX LERNER, AMERICAN JOURNALIST

———•••———

I've already lived about 20 years
longer than my life expectancy
at the time I was born. That's
a source of annoyance to
a great many people.

RONALD REAGAN

———•••———

In Liverpool, the difference
between a funeral and a
wedding is one less drunk.

PAUL O'GRADY

I know I can't cheat
death, but I can
cheat old age.

DARWIN DEASON, AMERICAN BUSINESSMAN

If you die in an elevator, be
sure to push the Up button.

SAM LEVENSON, AMERICAN WRITER AND COMEDIAN

———— •●• ————

Errol Flynn died on a 70-foot
yacht with a 17-year-old girl. My
husband's always wanted to go
that way, but he's going to settle
for a 17-footer and a 70-year-old.

BETSY CRONKITE, WIFE OF AMERICAN
JOURNALIST WALTER CRONKITE

———— •●• ————

Memorial services are
the cocktail parties of
the geriatric set.

HAROLD MACMILLAN, BRITISH PRIME MINISTER

My grandmother was a very tough woman. She buried three husbands and two of which were just napping.

RITA RUDNER

———•••———

I don't mind dying. Trouble is, you feel so bloody stiff the next day.

GEORGE AXELROD, AMERICAN SCREENWRITER, PRODUCER AND PLAYWRIGHT

———•••———

An old lady came into the chemist and asked for a bottle of euthanasia. I didn't say anything. I just handed her a bottle of Echinacea.

LYDIA BERRYMAN

I am ready to meet my Maker. Whether my Maker is ready for the ordeal of meeting me is another matter.

WINSTON CHURCHILL

A stockbroker urged me to buy a stock that would triple its value every year. I told him, 'At my age, I don't even buy green bananas.'

CLAUDE D. PEPPER, AMERICAN POLITICIAN

My old mam reads the obituary page everyday but she could never understand how people always die in alphabetical order.

FRANK CARSON, IRISH COMEDIAN AND ACTOR

Death is life's way of telling you you're fired.

ANONYMOUS

I don't believe in afterlife,
although I am bringing a
change of underwear.

WOODY ALLEN

———•●•———

They say such nice things about
people at their funerals that it
makes me sad that I'm going to
miss mine by just a few days.

GARRISON KEILLOR, AMERICAN WRITER AND BROADCASTER

———•●•———

The ageing process is not
gradual or gentle. It rushes up,
pushes you over and runs off
laughing. Dying is a matter
of slapstick and prat falls.

JOHN MORTIMER

Old age is like waiting
in the departure lounge
of life. Fortunately, we
are in England and the
train is bound to be late.

MILTON SHULMAN, CANADIAN WRITER AND DRAMA CRITIC

No one is so old as to think he cannot live one more year.

CICERO, ROMAN ORATOR AND PHILOSOPHER

———•●•———

Life insurance is a weird concept. You really don't get anything for it. It works like this: you pay me money and when you die, I'll pay you money.

BILL KIRCHENBAUER, AUSTRIAN-BORN AMERICAN COMEDIAN

———•●•———

If you think nobody cares whether you are alive or dead, try missing a couple of car payments.

ANN LANDERS, AMERICAN ADVICE COLUMNIST

WOMEN AND MEN

Trouble is, by the time
you can read a girl like
a book, your library
card has expired.

MILTON BERLE

Few women admit their
age. Few men act theirs.

ANONYMOUS

———•••———

An archaeologist is the best
husband a woman can have.
The older she gets the more
interested he is in her.

AGATHA CHRISTIE

———•••———

When women enter middle
age, it gives men a pause.

ANONYMOUS

The best years of a woman's life –
the ten years between 39 and 40.

ANONYMOUS

Women are not forgiven for
ageing. Robert Redford's
lines of distinction are
my old-age wrinkles.

JANE FONDA, AMERICAN ACTRESS

The lovely thing about
being 40 is that you can
appreciate 25-year-old men.

COLLEEN MCCULLOUGH, AUSTRALIAN
WRITER AND NEUROSCIENTIST

My husband's idea of a good
night out is a good night in.

**MAUREEN LIPMAN, BRITISH FILM, THEATRE AND
TELEVISION ACTRESS, COLUMNIST AND COMEDIAN**

———•••———

When I passed 40 I dropped
pretence, 'cause men like
women who got some sense.

MAYA ANGELOU, AMERICAN POET, MEMOIRIST AND ACTRESS

———•••———

Whatever you may look
like, marry a man your own
age – as your beauty fades,
so will his eyesight.

PHYLLIS DILLER

A woman's always younger
than a man of equal years.

ELIZABETH BARRETT BROWNING, BRITISH POET

———•••———

The best way to get a husband
to do anything is to suggest
that he is too old to do it.

FELICITY PARKER

———•••———

Age to women is like
Kryptonite to Superman.

KATHY LETTE, AUSTRALIAN WRITER

YOUTH V OLD AGE

The old begin to
complain of the
conduct of the young
when they themselves
are no longer able to
set a bad example.

FRANÇOIS DE LA ROCHEFOUCAULD

An old timer is one who remembers when we counted our blessings instead of our calories.

ANONYMOUS

———•••———

I am not young enough to know everything.

OSCAR WILDE

———•••———

Youth is a wonderful thing. What a crime to waste it on children.

GEORGE BERNARD SHAW

A man has reached middle age
when he is warned to slow down
by his doctor instead of the police.

ANONYMOUS

———•••———

I have now gotten to the age
when I must prove that I'm
just as good as I never was.

REX HARRISON, BRITISH ACTOR

———•••———

Young men want to be faithful,
and are not; old men want to
be faithless, and cannot.

OSCAR WILDE

I never dared to be radical when
young for fear it would make
me conservative when old.

ROBERT FROST

———•●•———

The elderly don't drive that
badly; they're just the only ones
with time to do the speed limit.

JASON LOVE, AMERICAN COMEDY WRITER

———•●•———

In youth we tend to look
forward; in old age we tend
to look back; in middle age
we tend to look worried.

ANONYMOUS

Young people don't know
what age is, and old people
forget what youth was.

IRISH PROVERB

———•●•———

The young man knows
the rules but the old man
knows the exceptions.

**OLIVER WENDELL HOLMES, AMERICAN PHYSICIAN,
WRITER AND HARVARD PROFESSOR**

———•●•———

In youth we run into
difficulties. In old age
difficulties run into us.

BEVERLY SILLS, AMERICAN OPERA SINGER

In youth the days are short and the years are long; in old age the years are short and the days are long.

NIKITA IVANOVICH PANIN, RUSSIAN STATESMAN

———●●●———

One of the many things nobody ever tells you about middle age is that it's a nice change from being young.

WILLIAM FEATHER

The old age of an eagle
is better than the
youth of a sparrow.

PROVERB

The old believe everything; the middle-aged suspect everything; the young know everything.

OSCAR WILDE

———•••———

Youth would be an ideal state if it came a little later in life.

HERBERT ASQUITH, EARL OF OXFORD AND ASQUITH, BRITISH PRIME MINISTER

Age is not different from earlier
life as long as you're sitting down.

MALCOLM COWLEY

——•••——

People want you to be like
you were in 1969. They want
you to be, because otherwise
their youth goes with you.

MICK JAGGER, BRITISH ROCK MUSICIAN

——•••——

Youth is when you're
allowed to stay up late on
New Year's Eve. Middle age
is when you're forced to.

BILL VAUGHN, AMERICAN INDUSTRY WRITER

I am getting older in a country
where a major religion is
the Church of Acne.

BILL COSBY

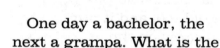

One day a bachelor, the
next a grampa. What is the
secret of the trick? How did
I get so old so quick?

OGDEN NASH

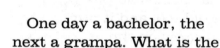

When you are dissatisfied and
would like to go back to your
youth... Think of algebra.

WILL ROGERS

From the earliest times the old
have rubbed it into the young
that they are wiser than they, and
before the young had discovered
what nonsense this was they
were old too, and it profited them
to carry on the imposture.

Somerset Maugham, British Playwright and Novelist

— ● ● —

I have everything I had 20 years
ago, only it's all a little bit lower.

Gypsy Rose Lee, American Actress
and Burlesque Entertainer

If you're interested in finding out more about our books, find us on Facebook at **Summersdale Publishers** and follow us on Twitter at **@Summersdale**.

www.summersdale.com